DISCOVER TOFU
A HEART TO HEART
COOKBOOK

1997
Published and distributed by

Magic Wings™
Post Office Box 9082
Calabasas, California
91372-9082

Printed in the United States of America

ISBN 0-9660605-0-4

IN LOVING MEMORY OF MY MOTHER

I dedicate this book to my mother Luise, who taught me at an early age how to cook; along with all the other arts of homemaking and gardening. I will remain grateful to her for those blessings.

My mother was a real magician when it came to food. Right after the war, food was scarce in Germany; our main staple was potatoes. Mother managed to cook potatoes in so many delicious ways, we always felt our meals to be of a great variety.

When she cooked there was a look of devotion on her face, one could see she enjoyed what she was doing. When she served the food a satisfied smile appeared; obviously she was pleased with her creation. My father's honest and diplomatic comment always was: "Niemand kann so gut kochen wie die mutter." ("No one can cook as good as mother.") Like magic, his words transformed her face into a beam of shining light. Oh the power of words, never should they be underestimated.

❤ to ❤

ACKNOWLEDGEMENTS

My deepest gratitude first and foremost goes to God, the giver of all good. Who makes me realize more and more as time goes by, that on my own I can do nothing. He is the doer!

Grateful acknowledgment to my family and friends for their support. Especially my daughter Cynthia and her husband Stuart. My two sons Ernie and Coy and Coy's wife Lilian. .

Nancy Clark, her husband Dr.Walter Clark and her mother Grace Golden.

Jennifer Otto, store owner of Healing Waters in L. A. Ca. She specializes in flower remedies and Aura-Soma color therapy.

Nancy Kitchen, director of the Payson Library at Pepperdine University.

Wally Wiesch, founder of Winners in Falls Church, Va.

Mark Labinger from the Bodhi Tree Bookstore in L. A. Ca.

Joe Righteous, Bill Jaynes and Maggie Mahboubian.

My thanks to Pepperdine's computer center and the local Libraries for their kind assistance.

Last, but not least; many thanks to the people in the supermarket who unknowingly inspired me to write this book.

❤ to ❤

PROLOGUE

Inspired by you! Let me share with you how this cook book came about. Many times when I purchased tofu at the supermarket, while waiting in the checkout line, people would ask me, "How do you cook tofu? What can you do with it?" Some would say, "My doctor asked me to include tofu into my diet, but it tastes so blah."

Many of us can relate to the inner battle which goes on between our good intentions and our demanding taste buds.

It is my intention to prove, that tofu can easily be included into our diet and can also be tasteful. In recipes tofu acts like a sponge and has the miraculous ability to soak up any flavor that is added to it. Note where recipes call for dairy or egg products, substitutes may be used.

Please consider the recipes in this book as guidelines and allow your imagination to roam. Enjoy - Bon Apetit!
❤ to ❤

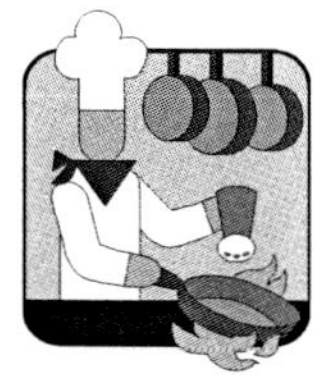

TABLE OF CONTENTS

IN MEMORY OF

ACKNOWLEDGEMENTS

PROLOGUE

TABLE OF CONTENTS

MISCELLANEOUS 1

DIPS AND SPREADS 5

SOUPS 13

SALADS 16

SALAD DRESSING 25

FILLINGS 27

SAUCES 31

MAIN DISH 36

DESSERTS 59

SOY FACTS 63

TIPS 64

INDEX 65

CATEGORY 66

<u>RECIPE FOR HAPPINESS</u>

1 Ounce Courage
1 Heaping Tablespoon Forgiveness
1 Cup Generosity
1 Cup Good Sense of Humor
1 Big Bright Smile
1 Bit Understanding
1 Pinch Kindness
Lots of Pure Honesty Extract

Mix all of the above with an unlimited amount of love. Slowly let it simmer in you r mind for 8 hours. For a stronger potency, simmer even longer.
❤ to ❤

Warning: Daily practice can become habit-forming
And prevent future worries.

BANANA & TOFU FOR BABIES

1/2 cup tofu*
1 ripe banana
honey to taste (optional)

Mash tofu and bananas, add honey.
*It is recommended to ask your doctor at what age your baby can start to eat tofu. Some babies have a reaction to honey, again best to first check with your doctor.
A great snack for any age.
❤ to ❤

"If thou canst believe, all things are possible to him that beliveth."

- Mark 9:23

BREAD CRUMBS

Cut your favorite bread into small squares and place on a cookie sheet, bake at 200° until bread is dry, approx. 1-2 hours. Mix in blender or crush by hand with roller.

For tofu recipes it is recommended to use a hearty bread; like rye with seeds, wheat berry, or oatnut. 6-7 large slices of bread will make approx. 1 cup of bread crumbs. Store in a closed container.
❤ to ❤

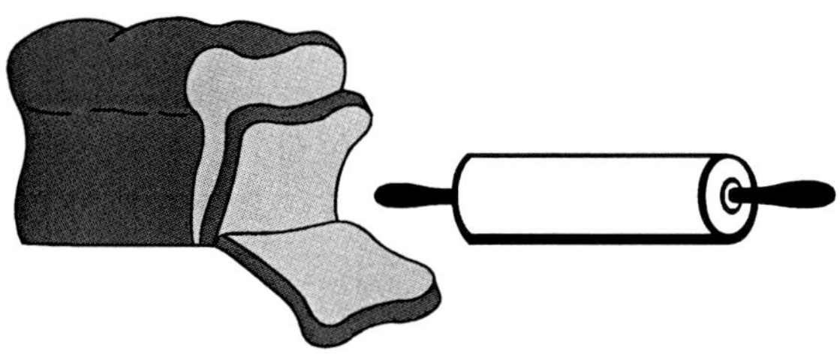

"Ingratitude is always a form of weakness. I have never known a man of real ability to be ungrateful."
- Johann Wolfgang Goethe

PIE CRUST

1 cup flour
1/4 cup margarine
1/4 tsp. apple cider vinegar
1/4 tsp. baking powder
1 cup & 1 tbsp. water
pinch of sugar
1/4 tsp. salt

Pour flour into bowl, with fork blend in margarine. Add remaining ingredients, mix thoroughly. Knead dough with your hands several minutes until you have a nice round and smooth ball. For best results, cover dough and keep in refrigerator for several hours or over-night. When ready to use, roll dough on a floured board to approx. 1/8" thickness. Fit dough into quiche or baking pan, pour in filling.
❤ to ❤

For recipe of quiche filling see index.

"We should be swift to carry out our resolutions, but slow in forming them."

- Aristotle

BAKED POTATO TOPPING

1/2 cup tofu
1/2 cup regular or nonfat sour cream*
1/2 cup green onions
2 tbsp. horseradish
spike to taste
salt to taste

.
Mash tofu and mix with remaining ingredients, leave green onions till last. Place tofu topping on baked or boiled potatoes, top with green onions. Optional: sprinkle with paprika.
*Non dairy can be used in place of dairy.
❤ to ❤

“Remember that miracles are made by people who can, because they think they can.”
- Norman Vincent Peale

BEAN & TOFU DIP

1 cup cooked beans, red (or your choice)
1/2 cup tofu
1 tbsp. nonfat sour cream*
2 tbsp. onions, chopped fine
1/4 tsp. onion powder
1/4 tsp. chili powder
1/4 tsp. cumin
spike to taste
salt to taste
fresh lemon or lime juice to taste

Mash beans and tofu, mix in remaining ingredients. Serve with assorted crackers, tortilla chips, cut-up vegetables, or spread on flour tortillas, roll up and cut into approx. 3/4" slices. *Non dairy sour cream can be used in place of dairy. Serves 2-3.
❤ to ❤

"Determine that the thing can and shall be done, and then we shall find a way."

- Abraham Lincoln

GUACAMOLE I.

1/2 cup tofu
1 cup avocado, soft
1 package guacamole mix (0.7 oz.)
1/2 cup nonfat or regular sour cream*
1/2 cup tomatoes, cut small
4 tbsp. green onions, cut small
fresh lemon or lime juice to taste
spike to taste
salt to taste

for extra spicy add: 1-2 tbsp. jalapeno peppers, minced

Mash avocado and tofu, mix till smooth. Add remaining ingredients, chill for 1 hour. Serve with chips, crackers, or fresh cut-up vegetables. *Non dairy sour cream can can be used in place of dairy. Serves 2-3.
❤ to ❤

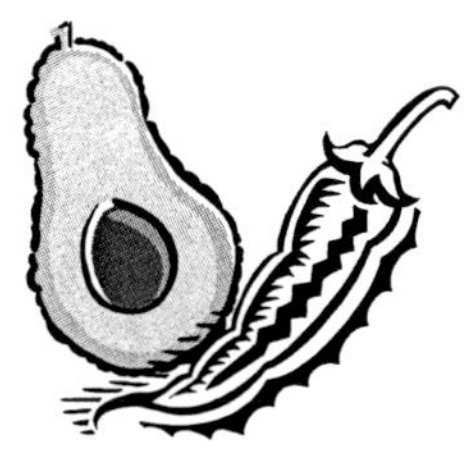

"Opportunities are usually disguised as hard work, so most people don't recognize them."
- Ann Landers

GUACAMOLE II.

1/2 cup tofu
1/2 cup avocado
1/2 cup nonfat sour cream
1/2 cup green onions, minced (optional)
2 tbsp. fresh lemon juice
1/8 tsp. garlic powder
1/8 tsp. onion powder
spike to taste
salt to taste

for extra spicy add: 1-2 tbsp. jalapeno peppers, minced

Mash avocado and tofu, mix till smooth. Add remaining Ingredients, chill for 1 hour. Serve with chips, assorted crackers, or fresh cut-up vegetables. Serves 2-3.
❤ to ❤

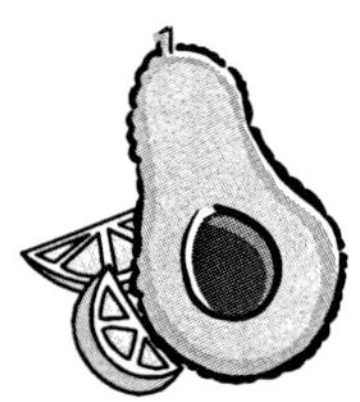

"I never did anything worth doing by accident, nor did any of my inventions come by accident; they came by work."

- Thomas A. Edison

HUMMUS

1cup garbanzo beans, drained
2/3 cup tofu
1 1/2 tbsp. fresh lime or lemon juice
1/4 cup juice from garbanzo beans
1/4 cup onions, chopped
1 large garlic clove, chopped
1/4 tsp. paprika
1/2 tsp. cumin
pinch of sugar
salt to taste
spike to taste
1 tsp. oil
1/4 cup sesame seeds, (optional)

1st. mix liquid, onions and garlic in blender. Add remaining ingredients (except sesame seeds), mix till mixture is smooth. Stir in sesame seeds. Place in serving b owl and chill before serving. Serve with crackers, fresh cut-up vegetables or tortilla chips. Serves 2-3.

❤ to ❤

"What is defeat? Nothing but education, nothing but the first step to something better."

- Wendell Phillips

ONION-TOFU DIP

1/2 cup tofu, mashed
1 cup regular or nonfat sour cream,*
fresh lemon juice to taste
2 tbsp. onion flakes
1/4 tsp. onion powder
1/4 tsp. garlic powder
1/8 tsp. paprika
salt to taste

Mix all ingredients well. Chill approx. 1-2 hours. Serve with chips, crackers or fresh cut-up vegetables. *Non dairy can be used in place of dairy. Serves 2.
❤ to ❤

"It is hard to fail, but it is worse never to have tried to succeed. In this life we get nothing save by effort."
- Theodore Roosevelt

PEANUTTO SPREAD

1/2 cup tofu
1/2 cup peanut butter, extra chunky
1/2 cup nonfat sour cream*

Mix all ingredients till smooth and creamy. Serve with your favorite toast or muffin. Tastes great on toasted wheatberry, or oatnut bread. Can also be used as a dip. Store in a closed container, keep refrigerated. *Non dairy can be used in place of dairy.

Other option: add 1/2 cup of date pieces. Let sit in refrigerator for a few hours or overnight, so the date pieces can expand. This makes a tasty and nutritious spread.
❤ to ❤

"Launch out into the deep - let the shoreline go."
- Unknown

TOFU-CHEESE BALL

1/2 cup tofu, mashed
1/2 cup nonfat ricotta cheese
1cup sharp cheddar cheese
1/2 cup green olives, chopped
1/4 cup pimentos, chopped
1/3 cup ground nuts of your choice
1 tsp. oregano leaves
1 -tsp. basil leaves
pinch of sugar
spike to taste
salt to taste

Mix all ingredients well, using only 2/3 of nuts. Form into a ball, roll ball in remaining nuts. Chill several hours before serving. Try also with sesame or poppy seeds.
❤ to ❤

"Real difficulties can be overcome; it is only the imaginary ones that are unconquerable."

- Theodore N. Vail

FLAEDLE SUPPE
(soup, german style)

1 pfannenkuchen II.*
(cut into 2"x 1/4" stripes)
1 cup tofu, cut into 1/4" squares
1 cup water
1 bouillon cube, of your choice
1/4 cup green onions, cut fine (optional)
* for recipe of pfannenkuchen II.
(pancakes, german style) see index)

Bring water to boil, add all ingredients.
Simmer 3-4 minutes. Serves 1-2.

"The best remedy for discontent is to count our blessings."
- Unknown

TOMATO SOUP I.
(quick)

1 can tomato soup (10 3/4 oz.)
1/2 cup water (for a thinner soup use 1 cup)
1/2 cup tofu, cut into 1/2" squares
1/4 cup onion flakes
1/4 tsp. oregano leaves*
1/4 cup nonfat sour cream
1/4 tsp. oil

Put all ingredients except sour cream in to a small pan, simmer 2-3 minutes. Add sour cream, simmer additional 1 minute. *Basil or dill can be used in place of oregano. Serve with crackers, toasted rye bread, or warm sour dough rolls. Serves 2-3.
❤ to ❤

"All experience is an arch to build upon."
- Henry Adams

TOMATO SOUP II
(hearty)

1 cup vegetables, cut (fresh or frozen)
1/4 cup onions, chopped small
1 can tomato soup (10 3/4 oz.)
1 cup water
1/2 cup rice, cooked
1 cup tofu, cut into 1/2" squares
1/4 cup nonfat sour cream
1/2 tsp. Oregano leaves*
1 tsp. oil for sauté

Sauté onions and vegetables in oil 4-5 minutes over medium heat. Add remaining ingredients, simmer additional 3-4 minutes. * Basil or dill can be used in place of oregano. Serve with crackers, toasted rye bread, or warm sour dough rolls Serves 3.
❤ to ❤

"A weak man becomes powerful when he is in contact with the mighty force of god."

- Unknown

CARROT & TOFU SALAD

1 cup carrots, cooked & diced
1/3 cup tomatoes, cut small
1/3 cup red pepper, cut small
1/2 cup tofu, cut into 1/4" squares
1/2 cup onions, chopped fine
1/3 cup italian dressing
salt to taste

Mix all ingredients, save tofu for last. Let chill 1-2 hours. Serves 2.
❤ to ❤

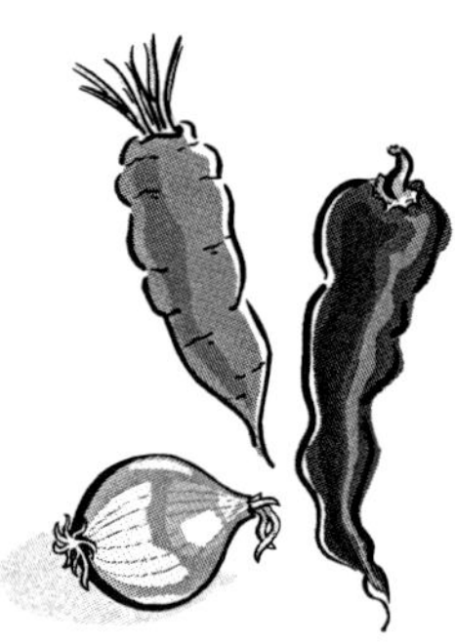

"Patience is needed with every one, but first of all with ourselves."
- Saint Francis de Sales

CUCUMBER-TOFU SALAD

1 cup cucumbers, diced small
1/2 cup tofu, crumbled
1/2 cup green onions, cut fine
1/4 cup nonfat yogurt*
1/4 cup nonfat sour cream*
1/4 cup black olives, sliced
1 tsp. fresh parsley, chopped fine**
1 tsp. fresh lemon or lime juice
1/4 tsp. onion powder
1/4 tsp. paprika
spike to taste
salt to taste

Gently mix all ingredients. *Non dairy can be used in place of dairy. ** Dill can be used in place of Parsley. Let chill 1-2 hours before serving. Serves 2.
❤ to ❤

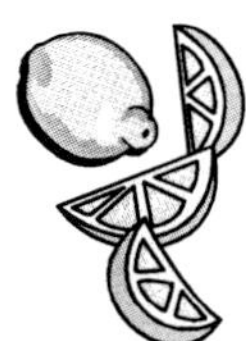

"In solitude we are least alone."
- Unknown

EGG & TOFU SALAD

1cup tofu, crumbled
4 hard boiled eggs, cut small
1 cup dill pickles, chopped fine
1cup black olives, sliced
4 tbsp. lowfat mayonnaise
2 tbsp. nonfat sour cream
1-2 tbsp. mustard
spike to taste
salt to taste

Gently mix all ingredients in a medium size bowl. Chill before serving. Sprinkle with paprika. Serves 2-3.
❤ to ❤

"Not failure, but low aim, is crime."
- James Russell Lowell

MUSHROOM & TOFU MARINADE

1cup tofu, diced into 1/2" squares
1/2 cup onions, chopped fine
1cup mushrooms, sliced
1 1/2 cup italian dressing

if you like to make your own dressing, see index for recipe of italian dressing.

Place tofu, mushrooms and onions in medium size bowl. Cover with italian dressing, marinate over night in refrigerator. Serve with a warm french sourdough roll or bread. Or mix into your favorite salad. Serves 2.
❤ to ❤

"Win without boasting. Lose without excuse."
- Albert Payson Terhune

PASTA & TOFU SALAD

2 cups pasta, cooked
1/4 cup black olives, sliced
1 cup carrots, cooked & sliced
1/2 cup green onions, cut small
1 cup mushrooms, sliced
1/2 cup red pepper, cut small
1 cup tofu, crumbled
3/4 cup italian dressing, use more if needet
spike to taste
salt to taste

Allow pasta and carrots to cool. Mix with remaining ingredients. Place in serving bowl, chill before serving. Rice can be used in place of pasta. Serves 3-4.
❤ to ❤

"It is not enough to have a good mind. The main thing is to use it well."

- Rene Descartes

ROTE RUEBEN & TOFU SALAT
(beet salad, german style)

2 cup beets, cooked & grated
1 cup tofu, crumbled
1/2 cup onions, chopped fine
2 tbsp. apple cider vinegar
1 tsp. sugar
1 tbsp. oil
salt to taste (very little)

Mix all ingredients well, chill before serving. Beets will turn tofu into a fuchsia color, lending the salad a festive and colorful look. Serves 2-3.
❤ to ❤

“My greatest inspiration is a challenge to attempt the impossible.”

- Albert A. Michelson

TABULE
(tabouli, lebanese style)

1/2 cup tofu, crumbled
1 cup tomatoes, cut small
1/4 cup green onions, cut fine
1 1/2 cup parsley, chopped fine
2 tbsp. fresh mint, chopped fine
2 tbsp. fresh lemon or lime juice
1 tbsp. wheat germ (optional)
2 tbsp. olive oil
pepper to taste
salt to taste

Mix all ingredients in a medium size serving bowl. Chill 1 - 2 hours before serving. Serves 2.
❤ to ❤

"The greater the difficulty the more glory in surmounting it."
- Epicurus

TART'LY TOFU

1 cup tofu, crumbled
1/2 cup onions, chopped fine
1/2 cup dill pickles, chopped fine
1/2 cup green olives with pimento, chopped fine
1/4 cup lowfat italian dressing
1 tbsp. fresh lemon juice
salt to taste

Mix all ingredients in a medium size bowl. To marinate tofu, cover bowl and let sit several hours or overnight in refrigerator.

1/2 cup water
1envelope plain gelatin
Pour gelatin over cold water in a small saucepan. Over low heat bring to a boil, stir constantly until gelatin is dissolved. Remove from heat and mix with tofu mixture.
Chill until firm. Serves 2-3.
❤ to ❤

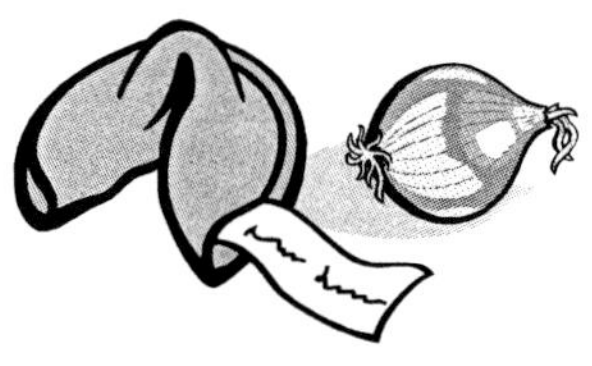

"Virtue is not hereditary."
- Thomas Paine

TOMATO & TOTU SALAD

1 cup tomatoes, cut
1/4 cup tofu, crumbled
1/4 cup regular or nonfat sour cream*
1/4 cup onions, cut small
(green or regular)
fresh lemon juice to taste
spike to taste
salt to taste

Gently mix all ingredients and place in serving dish.
*Non dairy can be used in place of dairy.

6 black olives, sliced
dash of paprika
Sprinkle salad with paprika and decorate with sliced olives. Serves 1-2.
❤ to ❤

"There can be no rainbow without a cloud and a storm."
- John Heyl Vincent

ITALIAN DRESSING

1/2 cup onions, chopped fine
2 garlic cloves, chopped fine
1 tsp. fresh rosemary, chopped fine
2 tbsp. apple cider vinegar
1 tbsp. fresh lemon juice
1/8 tsp. paprika
2 tbsp. water
2 tsp. sugar
2 tbsp. oil
salt to taste
spike to taste

For best results, store in a closed jar and keep in the Refrigerator 1-2 days. Makes approx. 2/3 cups
❤ to ❤

"Ideas control the world."
- James A. Garfield

TOFRUITY
(for fruit salad)

1/2 cup tofu, mashed
1/2 cup nonfat yogurt or sour cream*
1/2 cup coconut milk
2 tsp. rosewater, fresh lemon juice
sugar or honey to taste

Mix all ingredients in blender. Keep in refrigerator until ready to use. Dressing can be used with any combination of fruits. *Non dairy can be used in place of dairy
Makes 1 1/2 cups.
Where to find coconut milk and rosewater? See tips.
❤ to ❤

"Let there be space in your togetherness"
- Kahlil Gibran

COTTAGE CHEESE & TOFU FILLING

1/2 cup tofu, mashed
1/2 cup lowfat cottage cheese
2 tbsp. nonfat sour cream
dash of salt

use this filling with pfannenkuchen I.
(pancakes, german style) For recipe see index.

Mix above ingredients well.
Spread mixture on pfannenkuchen and top with jam, or fresh fruit, or sugar and cinnamon. Fold or roll and serve. Filling for 4 pfannenkuchen I.
(pancakes, german style).

"Often it does seem such a pity, that Noah and his party did not miss the boat."

\- Mark Twain

ENCHILADA FILLING

1/2 cup jack cheese, shredded*
1/2 cup sharp cheddar cheese, shredded*
(3 tbsp. extra for topping)
1/2 cup tofu, mashed
1/2 cup green onions chopped fine
1/2 cup nonfat sour cream *
1 cup black olives, sliced
1/4 tsp. onion powder
salt to taste
8 corn tortillas
for recipe of enchilada sauce see index

In a medium size bowl, mix tofu with cheese, seasoning and olives. Save sour cream and onions for topping. Dip each sautéed or plain tortilla in sauce, place filling in center and roll. Place seam side down in baking dish. Pour rest of sauce over enchiladas, sprinkle with remaining cheese. Cover with foil, bake approx. 20-25 minutes at 350°. Remove foil, top with sour cream and onions, bake additional 5-10 minutes.
Serves 4.
Non dairy cheese/sour cream can be used in place of dairy.
❤ to ❤

"Kites rise highest against the wind not with it."
- Winston Churchill

LASAGNE FILLING

1/2 cup tofu
1/2 cup ricotta cheese
1/3 cup sharp cheddar cheese, shredded
1/3 cup jack cheese, shredded
1/3 cup mozzarella cheese, shredded
1/2 cup regular or nonfat sour cream
1/4 tsp. garlic powder
1/2 tsp. basil
salt to taste
spike to taste
for recipe of lasagne sauce see index

Mix all ingredients in medium size bowl, keep in refrigerator till ready to use.
1/2 box lasagne
To cook lasagne noodles: follow directions on package. Cover bottom of an 8 x 8" baking dish with small amount of sauce. Layer alternately as follows: 1 layer noodles, 1 layer filling, 1 layer sauce. Repeat layers. Sauce should be last. Cover dish and bake at 350° for 40 minutes. Remove cover and bake additional 5-7 minutes. Serves 4.
❤ to ❤

"A man can succeed at almost anything for which he has unlimited enthusiasm."

- Charles Schwab

MUSHROOM-TOFU FILLING*

1 cup tofu, crumbled
1 cup onions, chopped fine
2 cups mushrooms, cut small
1/4 cup nonfat sour cream (optional)
oil for sauté
salt to taste
spike to taste

use this filling with pfannenkuchen II.
(pancakes, german style) For recipe see index.
*This filling can also be used as a topping on pasta or rice.

Sauté onions in oil, approx. 5 minutes over medium heat. Add mushrooms, tofu and spices; sauté additional 5 minutes. Add sour cream last. Spread mixture on pfannenkuchen, fold or roll and serve. Filling for 4-5 pfannenkuchen II. (pancakes, german style).
❤ to ❤

"Always do right; this will gratify some people and astonish the rest."

- Mark Twain

CHILI SAUCE
(with tofu)

1 can crushed tomatoes (14 1/2 oz.)
1/2 package chili seasoning mix
1 cup tofu, cut into 1/2" squares
1/4 cup onions, chopped fine*
1 tbsp. brown sugar
1/2 cup water
1 tsp. Oil

Sauté onions in oil, add remaining ingredients, saving tofu for last. Heat in saucepan, simmer on low heat for 10 minutes. Add plain or sautéed tofu squares, cook additional 2-3 minutes. *Onion flakes can be used in place of fresh onions. Serve with rice, beans or pasta. Serves 2-3.
❤ to ❤

"Shallow men believe in luck. Strong men believe in cause and effect."

- Ralph Waldo Emerson

ENCHILADA SAUCE

1 package enchilada sauce mix (1.62 oz.)
1 can crushed tomatoes (28 oz,)
1 can tomato sauce (8 oz.)
1 bouillon cube of your choice
2 cup water
1 large garlic clove, minced
1/2 tsp. thyme leaves
1/2 tsp. oregano leaves
1/4 tsp. sugar
spike to taste
salt to taste
for recipe of enchilada filling see index

Pour all ingredients in medium size pan. Mix and stir, bring to boil. Reduce heat, simmer approx. 15-20 minutes.
❤ to ❤

"If you think you can, or if you think you can't - you're right."

- Henry Ford

LASAGNE SAUCE

1 can tomatoes, crushed (28 oz.)
1 small can tomato sauce (8 oz.)
1 cup mushrooms, sliced
1 cup onions, chopped small
1/2 tsp. basil leaves
1 1/2 tsp. oregano leaves
2 bouillon cubes of your choice
2 garlic cloves, chopped
1/2 tsp. sugar
spike to taste
salt to taste
oil for sauté
for recipe of filling see index

In a medium size pan, sauté onions in oil till golden brown. Mix with remaining ingredients, bring to boil, let simmer on low heat for 20 minutes. Serves 4.
❤ to ❤

"Why not go out on a limb? That's where the fruit is."
- Unknown

MEERRETTICH SOSSE
(horseradish sauce, german style)

3 tbsp. margarine or oil
2 tbsp. flour
2 tbsp. fresh lemon juice
1 egg yolk
2 tbsp. horseradish, prepared
1 cup lowfat or regular milk*
1 tbsp. nonfat or regular Sour Cream*
small pinch of sugar
salt to taste

Melt margarine in fry pan; sauté flour till golden brown. Slowly pour in milk and add egg yolk, bring to a boil while constantly stirring. Reduce heat to low, add remaining ingredients and simmer approx. 2 minutes. Serves 2.
*Non dairy can be used in place of dairy.
Serve with salzkartoffel (potatoes german style) and tofu.

6 slices tofu, approx. 1/2" to 3/4" thick, sautéed
Place sautéed tofu slices on potatoes, pour sauce over top.
For recipe of salzkartoffel: see index.
❤ to ❤

"Great achievement demands great risks."
- Herodotus

TARTAR SAUCE
(with tofu)

1/4 cup dill pickles, chopped fine
1/4 cup onions, chopped fine
1/2 cup non or lowfat mayonnaise
1 1/2 tsp. lemon juice
pepper to taste
salt to taste

Mix all ingredients well. Let chill 1-2 hours.

6 slices tofu approx. 1/4" thick
Top cold tofu slices with tartar sauce, ready to serve.
Serves 2-3.
❤ to ❤

"One of the best ways to persuade others is with your ears-by listening to them."

- Dean Rusk

B • B • Q TOFU

4-6 slices of tofu, approx. 1/4" thick
1/2 cup b.b.q sauce
1/2 cup onions, chopped fine
3-4 large mushrooms, sliced

Layer in small baking dish as follows:
1. small amount of sauce on bottom
2. layer of onions
3. layer of tofu
4. layer of onions

pour over remaining sauce and place mushrooms on top.

Cover baking dish, keep in refrigerator several hours or overnight. When ready to cook, heat oven and bake at 375° 15-20 minutes. Can also be cooked on stove top or grill. Serves 2-3.
❤ to ❤

"What would life be like if we had no courage to attempt anything."

- Vincent Van Gosh

BURRITOS

1/2 cup tofu, crumbled
1/2 cup rice, cooked
1/2 cup beans, cooked & mashed
1/2 cup onions, chopped
1/4 cup tomatoes, chopped
1 tsp. flour
1/8 tsp. chili powder
1/2 tsp. oregano leaves
1/4 tsp. cumin
1/4 tsp. sugar
spike to taste
salt to taste
oil for cooking

Sauté onions and flour in oil till golden brown. Add tofu, beans, rice and spices. Cook approx. 2-3 minutes. Add tomatoes, cook additional 1 minute.
2 large tortillas
2 tbsp. sharp cheddar cheese, shredded
Heat tortillas in broiler or fry pan. Spread mixture in center, sprinkle with cheese and roll. Ready to serve. Serves 2.
❤ to ❤

Life is either a daring adventure or nothing at all."
- Helen Keller

CORN & TOFU MUSH

1/4 cup corn meal
1/2 cup tofu, crumbled
1/2 cup onions, chopped small
1 cup water
2 tsp. oil, butter or margarine
1/4 tsp. sage
salt to taste

Sauté onions in oil or margarine till light brown. Add corn meal, sauté additional 2 minutes. Add water and seasoning bring to boil while stirring. Reduce heat, add tofu, and let simmer for 5 minutes. Makes a quick, tasty and satisfying meal. Serves 1.
❤ to ❤

"As a man thinketh in his heart, so is he."
- Proverbs 23:7

CREAM OF WHEAT & TOFU

1 cup lowfat or regular milk*
1 cup water
1/3 cup cream of wheat
1/2 cup tofu, mashed
1 ripe banana, mashed
1/4 cup ground almonds
2 tbsp. sugar
1 tsp. butter or margarine
1/4 tsp. cinnamon
1/4 tsp. cardamon
1/8 tsp. nutmeg
salt to taste

Bring milk and water to a boil. Reduce heat, while stirring add cream of wheat. Cook for the amount of time indicated on package. Add remaining ingredients, cook additional 2 minutes. Makes a quick, tasty and nutritious meal for young and old. *Non dairy can be used in place of dairy. Serves 2.
❤ to ❤

"Destiny is no matter of chance, it is a matter of choice: it is not a thing to be waited for, it is a thing to be achieved."
- William Jennings Bryan

CURRY & TOFU CHOWDER

1 package tofu (14 oz.) cut into 1/2" squares
2 cup potatoes, peeled raw, cut into 3/4" squares
1 cup zucchini, cut small
1 cup carrots, cut small
3 cup cabbage, chopped small
1 cup onions, chopped fine
2 bouillon's of your choice
2 cup water
1 tbsp. curry
1/2 tbsp. cardamon
1/2 tbsp. coriander
1/2 tbsp. sugar
1 tbsp. oil
salt to taste

Boil potatoes and onions for approx. 10 minutes over medium heat. Add carrots, cabbage and spices; boil additional 10 minutes. Add zucchini, oil and tofu. Cook 5-7 minutes longer.
Serves 6-7
❤ to ❤

"Diligence is the mother of good luck."
- Benjamin Franklin

GARBANTO PATTY

1 cup garbanzo beans, mashed
1 cup tofu, crumbled
2 eggs (or egg substitute)
3/4 cup bread crumbs (rye with seeds)
1/2 cup onions, chopped fine
1/2 cup parsley, chopped fine
1 tsp. basil or oregano leaves
1tsp. flour
spike to taste
salt to taste
oil for frying

Mix ingredients well . Form into patties and place in hot greased fry pan. Cook both sides over medium heat till golden brown and done. Makes 7-8 patties.
Serve with pasta, rice, salad or vegetables.

Other option:: to make a loaf, place mixture in greased baking dish, cover with foil and bake at 375° approx. 25-30 minutes. Remove foil, bake additional 10 minutes.
❤ to ❤

"The mind grows on what it feeds."
- J.G. Holland

KARTOFFEL PUFFER
(potato puffs, german style)

1/2 cup tofu, mashed
1 cup potatoes, cooked & mashed
1/2 cup bread crumbs
1/4 cup onions, chopped fine
1/4 cup parsley, chopped fine
2 eggs
2 tbsp. flour
1 tsp. marjoram
salt to taste
spike to taste
1/4 tsp. baking powder*, (optional)
oil for frying

Mix all ingredients well; make medium size patties and place in greased hot fry pan. Cook over medium heat until done and each side is golden brown. Makes approx. 8-10 patties.
*For puffier patties use baking powder.
❤ to ❤

"The great use of life is to spend it for something that outlasts it."

- William James

MUSHROOM-TOFU PATTY

1 cup tofu, crumbled
1 cup mushrooms, chopped small
1/4 cup ground nuts, filbert & almond mix
(or of your choice)
1/2 cup bread crumbs (rye with seeds)
1/2 cup onions, chopped fine
2 tsp. worcestershire or soy sauce sauce
1/4 tsp. onion powder
2 eggs (or egg substitute)
1 tbsp. flour
spike to taste
salt to taste
oil for frying

Mix ingredients well, add mushrooms last. Form into medium size patties, place in hot greased fry pan. Cook both sides over medium heat till golden brown and done. Makes approx. 8 patties. Serve with pasta, rice, salad or vegetables.
❤ to ❤

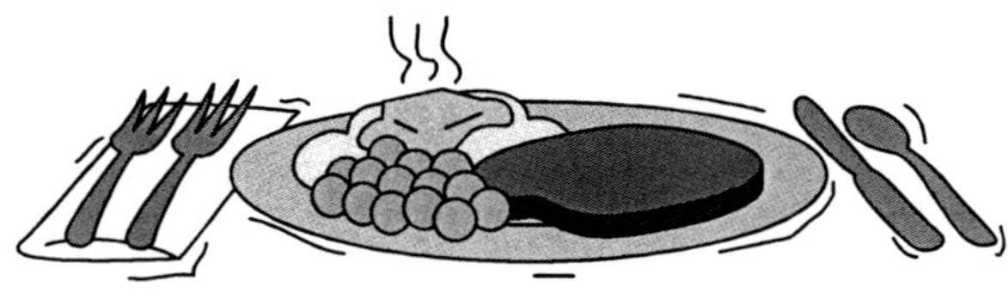

"Do you want to succeed? Then, double your rate of failure Success lies on the far side of failure."

\- Thomas J. Wilson

OMELET

2 eggs (or egg substitute)
1/2 cup tofu, mashed
1/4 cup mushrooms, sliced
1/4 cup cheddar or swiss cheese, shredded*
1/4 cup green or regular onions, chopped small
2 tbsp. milk*
spike to taste
salt to taste
oil, margarine or butter for frying

Beat eggs and milk in a small bowl, mix with remaining ingredients. Pour into greased hot omelet pan. Cook over low-medium heat, each side approx. 3-4 minutes, until done. *Non dairy can be used in place of dairy. Serves 1-2.

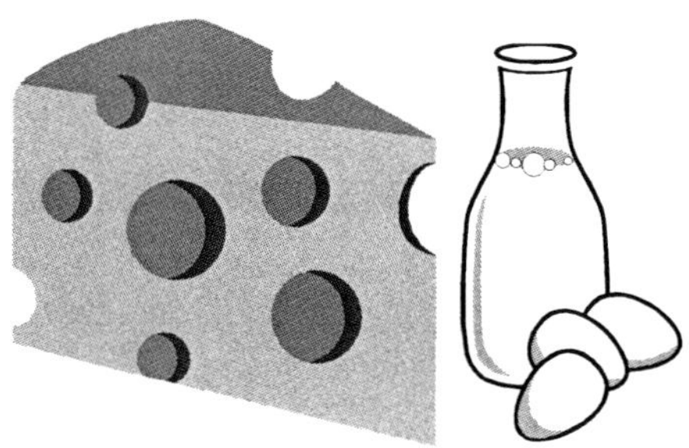

"Change your thoughts and you can change your world."
- Norman Vincent Peale

PARMESAN a la TOFU

6 slices tofu, firm or extra firm (approx. 1/2" thick)
1 egg (or egg substitute)
1 1/2 tbsp. flour
2/3 cups bread crumbs (rye with seeds)
4 tbsp. parmesan cheese
1 tbsp. oregano leaves
1/4 cup fresh parsley, chopped fine
1/2 lowfat mozzarella, shredded*
1 cup chunky spaghetti sauce
1 cup tomatoes, cut fine
salt to taste
spike to taste
oil for baking,

Dredge tofu in flour, dip in egg. In separate bowl mix bread Crumbs, parmesan cheese and seasoning. Place tofu slices in greased 8 x 8" baking dish, pour over remaining egg. Sprinkle with bread crumbs mixture, bake with cover at 375° approx. 20 minutes. Remove cover, top with spaghetti sauce, tomatoes and mozzarella. Bake additional 20 minutes. *Non dairy can be used in place of dairy. Serves 3-4.
❤ to ❤

"The creation of a thousand forests is in one acorn."
- Ralph Waldo Emerson

PFANNENKUCEN I.
(pancakes, german style)

1 cup flour
2 eggs (or egg substitute)
1/2 cup water or milk*
salt to taste
oil for frying
for a crisper pancake use water.

Mix all ingredients except oil, in electric mixer. Pour batter into greased, hot 10" fry pan, enough to coat bottom. Tilt pan to spread evenly. Reduce heat, cook until both sides are golden brown. Makes 4 pfannenkuchen. *Non dairy milk can be used in place of regular. Serves 2.
❤ to ❤

For filling use: cottage cheese & tofu filling.
See index for recipe.

"Mind has its influence on mind; and no man is free but when alone."

\- M. Tupper

PFANNENKUCHEN II.
(pancakes, german style)

1 cup flower
2 eggs (or egg substitute)
1/2 cup water
1 tsp. apple cider vinegar
1/4 cup parsley, chopped fine
1/4 cup green onions, cut small
oil for frying
salt to taste

Mix all ingredients except oil, in electric mixer. Pour batter into greased, hot 10" fry pan, enough to coat bottom. Tilt pan to spread evenly. Reduce heat, cook until both sides are golden brown. Makes 4 pfannenkuchen. Serves 2.
❤ to ❤

For filling use mushroom & tofu filling.
See index for recipe.

"We are confronted with insurmountable opportunities."
- Pogo

QUICHE

1 cup tofu, crumbled
1 cup swiss or cheddar cheese, shredded*
2 cup mushrooms, sliced
1 tbsp. parmesan cheese
1 tbsp. fresh parsley, chopped fine
1 cup onions, chopped fine
4 eggs (or egg substitute)
1 tsp. basil
1/2 tsp. thyme
1 1/2 tbsp., flour
1 1/2 tbsp. oil
spike to taste
salt to taste
for recipe of pie crust see index.

Sauté onions in oil, approx. 5 minutes. Add mushrooms and flour sauté additional 5 minutes. In a big bowl beat eggs, add all ingredients and mix well. Pour into a 9" quiche or baking pan. Bake at 350° approx. 35 - 40 minutes.
*Non dairy can be used of place of dairy).
❤ to ❤

"If life were predictable, it would cease to be life and be without flavor."

- Eleanor Roosevelt

ROT KRAUT & TOFU
(red cabbage, german style)

6 cups red cabbage, chopped
2 cups apples, peeled & cut
1/2 cup onions, chopped
2 tbsp. apple cider vinegar
1 cup water
1 tbsp. sugar
2 bay leaves
7 cloves
2 tbsp. oil
salt to taste

In a large cooking pot, sauté onions in oil until light brown. Add remaining ingredients, bring to a boil. Reduce heat, simmer 45-50 minutes. Serves 5-6.
❤ to ❤

2-3 slices of tofu per person, approx. 1/4" thick
Sauté tofu, till both sides are golden brown. Serve with rot kraut (red cabbage) and salzkartoffel (potatoes german style).
For recipe of salzkartoffell see index.

"We all boil at different degrees."
- Ralph Waldo Emerson

SALZKARTOFFEL
(potatoes, german style)

3 cups potatoes, raw
1/3 cup water
salt to taste

Peel potatoes and cut into approx. 1" squares. In medium size pot bring water and potatoes to a boil. Reduce heat, cook approx. 20 minutes or until done. Serves 2.

Salzkartoffel, go well with meerrettich sosse (horseradish sauce) and sauerkraut. For a quick meal: sauté 1 cup chopped onions and 1 cup crumbled tofu in oil or margarine, and place on top of potatoes. Guten Appetit.

"The difficult is that which can be done immediately; the impossible that which takes a little longer."
- George Santayana

SAUERKRAUT & TOFU
(sauerkraut, german style)

6-8 slices of tofu, approx. 1/4" thick
1 can sauerkraut, * drained (27 oz.)
1 1/2 cup onions, chopped fine
1 1/2 cup potatoes, raw & grated
1/2 tsp. Caraway seeds (optional)
oil for frying
1 tsp. Sugar
salt to taste

Sauté onions and potatoes in oil until golden brown. Remove from stove and mix in remaining ingredients. In a medium size baking dish place half amount of sauerkraut mixture, 1 layer tofu, then cover tofu with remaining sauerkraut mixture.

Cover baking dish with foil and bake at 375 ° for 20 minutes. Remove foil, bake additional 10 minutes.
If cooked on stove top, add small amount of water. Cooking time approx. 20 minutes. Baking however, will lend a richer flavor.
To save nutrients, sauerkraut should not be washed.
To make a drink, mix juice from sauerkraut with some water. Chill and serve.
❤ to ❤

"When we can dream no longer we die."
- Emma Goldman

SCRAMBLED EGGS & TOFU

2 eggs (or egg substitute)
1/2 cup onions, green or regular, cut small
1/2 cup mushrooms, sliced
1/2 cup tofu, crumbled
2 tsp. lowfat milk *
spike to taste
salt to taste
oil , butter or margarine for frying

In a small bowl beat eggs with milk, add remaining ingredients. Pour into greased hot fry pan, cook over Medium heat till done. *Non dairy milk can be used in place of dairy. Serves 1-2.
❤ to ❤

'The men who try to do something and fail are infinitely better than those who try to do nothing and succeed."
- Loyd Jones

SESAME-TOFU PATTY

1 cup tofu, mashed
3 tsp. worcestershire s or soy sauce
1/2 cup onions, chopped fine
1/2 cup corn bread dressing
1/2 cup zucchini, grated
1/2 cup fresh parsley, chopped fine
2 tbsp. sesame seeds
1 egg (or egg substitute)
2 tsp. flour
1/2 tsp. sage
1/2 tsp. marjoram
1/2 tsp. garlic powder
spike to taste
salt to taste
oil for frying

Mix ingredients well. Form into patties and place in greased hot fry pan. Cook both sides over medium heat till golden brown and done. Makes 6 -7 patties. Serve with pasta, rice, salad or vegetables.
❤ to ❤

"Good judgment comes from experience, and experience- well that comes from poor judgment."

- Unknown

STIR FRY

1/2 cup zucchini, cut
1/2 cup string beans, cut
1/2 cup carrots, cut
1/2 cup snow peas
1 cup mushrooms, sliced
1 cup onions, chopped
1 tsp. basil
spike to taste
salt to taste
oil for frying
1 cup tofu, cut into 1/2" squares

Sauté onions in greased hot fry pan till golden brown. Add vegetables and spices, sauté 3-4 minutes. Add tofu, cook additional 3-4 minutes. Serve with rice or pasta. Serves 3.
❤ to ❤

Other option: create a creamy style dish by adding 1 small can of mushroom soup and 1/4 cup nonfat sour cream. If to thick, add some water.

"There is no instinct like that of the heart."
- Unknown

TOFU CUTLET

6 slices tofu firm, approx. 1/4" thick
1 egg (or egg substitute)
2 tbsp. milk
dash oregano
dash onion salt
spike to taste
salt to taste
1/2 cup bread crumbs (rye with seeds)
oil for frying

Beat egg with milk, add spices. Pour bread crumbs into a separate bowl. 1. Dry each slice of tofu in a paper towel, to remove excess moisture. 2. Dip in egg batter. 3. Gently turn over in bread crumbs.
Place breaded slices in hot greased fry pan, cook over medium heat till both sides are golden brown and done.
Serves 2-3.
❤ to ❤

"Make the best of what is in your power, and take the rest as it happens."

- Epictetus

TORTILLAS EXCELENTE
(quick, nutritious & delicious)

4 corn tortillas
1/3 cup avocado, mashed
1/3 cup tofu, mashed
1/3 cup sharp cheddar cheese,* shredded
1/2 cup green onions, cut fine
2/3 cup tomatoes, cut small
1/2 tsp. fresh lemon or lime juice
dash onion powder
dash garlic powder
salt to taste
spike to taste

Mix tofu with avocados, spices and lemon juice. Spread mixture evenly on tortillas, place in broiler till light brown. It will take only a few minutes to heat and brown tortillas, so keep a close watch. Remove from broiler sprinkle with cheese, tomatoes and onions. Fold and serve.
*Non dairy can be used in place of dairy. Serves 2.
❤ to ❤

"The person who really thinks learns quite as much from his failures as from his successes."
- John Dewey

YAM & TOFU DELIGHT

1/2 cup tofu
1 cup yams, cooked
1/2 cup regular or nonfat sour cream*
1/2 cup brown sugar
1/2 tsp. cardamon
1/2 tsp. cinnamon
1/2 tsp. nutmeg
1 egg
1 tsp. oil
salt to taste
1/2 cup shredded coconuts (optional)

Mash tofu and yam, add remaining ingredients and beat with electric mixer till smooth. Pour mixture into a greased baking pan, bake at 375° approx. 45 minutes or until done. .
*Non dairy can be used in place of dairy. Serves 2.

Can also be used as a pie filling. For recipe of pie crust see index.
❤ to ❤

"The greatest events - are not our noisiest, but our stillest hours."

- Friedrich Nietzche

ZUCCHINI & TOFU CASSEROLE

1 1/2 cup onions, chopped fine
2 cups carrots, grated
4 cups zucchini cut into small chunks
2 cups cornbread dressing, seasoned
1/2 cup cream of mushroom soup
1/2 cup regular or nonfat sour cream*
1 container tofu 14" size, crumbled
2 tbsp. flour
1 tsp. basil leaves
1 tsp. Sage leaves
1 tsp. marjoram
1 tsp. thyme
1 tsp. spike
salt to taste
oil for sauté and baking

Sauté onions in oil for 5 minutes. Add carrots and flour, sauté additional 5 minutes. In a separate big bowl, mix sautéed onions and carrots with remaining ingredients. Place mixture in one large 15x10", or 2 medium size 8x8" baking dish, cover with foil and bake at 375 ° approx. 50 minutes. Remove cover and bake additional 10 minutes. *Non dairy can be used in place of dairy. Serves 5-6.
❤ to ❤

"Genius is one percent inspiration and ninety-nine percent perspiration."

- Thomas Edison

ALMONDTO PUDDING

1 cup tofu
1 cup nonfat ricotta cheese
1/2 cup ground almonds
1/3 cup sugar
2 tbsp. rosewater
tiny pinch of salt

Mix all ingredients well. Chill 1-2 hours before serving.

Fruit topping, (optional)
Top with sliced bananas, place berries or berry jam in center. Serves 2-3.
❤ to ❤

"To every thing there is a season, and a time to every purpose under the heaven."

- Ecclesiastes 3:1.

CHOCOLATE T MINT PUDDING
(quick and easy)

1 package instant chocolate pudding (3 1/8 oz.)
1/2 cup tofu
3/4 cup lowfat or regular milk*
1/4 tsp. mint extract

Mix tofu and milk in blender till smooth. Pour into a bowl, add pudding and mint extract, mix thoroughly. Chill 1-2 hours. *Non dairy can be used in place of dairy. Serves 2.
❤ to ❤

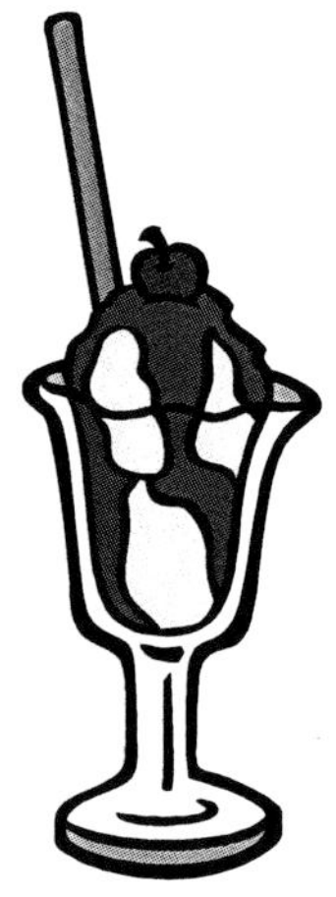

"Hitch your wagon to a star."
- Ralph Waldo Emerson

CRANBERRY & TOFU GELATIN

1/2 cup tofu
1/2 cup whole cranberry sauce (from can)
3/4 cup water
1 package sugar free raspberry gelatin (.32oz.)
1 tsp. orange marmalade
1 tsp. fresh ginger, chopped fine.
pinch of salt

In a medium size bowl, mash tofu and mix with cranberry sauce. In a separate bowl, mix gelatin with boiling water, until gelatin is completely dissolved. Combine all ingredients. Pour into serving dish, keep in refrigerator until firm. Approx. 1-2 hours. Serves 2-3.
❤ to ❤

"Love sees what no eyes see; love hears what no ears hear."
- Unknown

VANILLA-TOFU PUDDING
(quick & easy)

1 package instant vanilla pudding (3 1/8 oz.)
1/2 cup tofu
3/4 cup lowfat milk*
1/4 tsp. orange extract

Mix tofu and milk in blender till smooth. Pour into a bowl, add pudding mix and orange extract.
Mix thoroughly with wire wisk, pour immediately into desert dishes. Chill 1-2 hours.
*Non dairy can be used in place of dairy. Serves 2.
❤ to ❤

"I would rather be on the side of those who believe anything possible."

- Amelia Earhart

SOY FACTS

Today, farmers in over 29 states grow soybeans, making soybeans our second largest crop in cash value. "What a thought, by eating tofu we improve our health and at the same time support our farmers."

- Soybeans are the only vegetable food that contain complete protein.
- Menopausal woman who were fed soy, had almost 50 percent reduction in symptoms.
- Soy protein, a highly digestible source of amino acids.
- Soy protein, a source in infant formulas, athletic and health food supplements.
- Soy protein ranks as high as the protein in meat and milk.
- Scientists have identified several potential anticancer substances in soybeans.
- As little as one serving of soy foods each day, seems to protect against many types of cancer.
- Soy foods provide a unique way to improve bone health.
- Tofu, a good source of B-vitamins and iron.
- Tofu, low in saturated fat, contains no cholesterol.
- Tofu is also low in sodium, making it the perfect food for people on sodium restricted diets.
- More than 40 studies have found that adding soy protein to the diet lowers blood cholesterol.
- Soy foods, a natural source of daidzein could help reduce the risk of osteoporosis.

Calories in 4 ounce tofu will vary slightly, depending on type of tofu and manufacturer. Calories listed below are approximate, for accurate count please check label on tofu package.

	FIRM TOFU	REGULAR TOFU	SOFT TOFU
CALORIES:	120	95	86

Soy facts and nutritional information on this page, were generously provided by the American Soybean Association. FOR MORE INFORMATION ON SOYBEANS AND TOFU CALL 1-800-TALK-SOY.

TIPS

COCONUT MILK: made from coconuts, can be found in Middle-Eastern stores, international or gourmet section of some supermarkets, or health food stores.

DATE PIECES: dates rolled in oat flour, will expand when mixed with tofu. They lend tofu a natural sweetness. To be found at Trader Joe's, health food stores and some supermarkets.

HORSERADISH:
Is a white root, a plant of the mustard family. Most common used is the shredded relish style, which comes in small jars. With its pungent taste, horseradish adds zest to dips & sauces. To be found in the delicatessen or produce section of your Supermarket.

IN PLACE OF NONFAT: salad dressing, sour cream, yogurt etc., regular or lowfat can be used, if you prefer their taste and do not mind the calories.

ROSE WATER: made from rose extract and water, is used in desserts. Most common in Europe and Middle-Eastern countries. Lends food a subtle and delightful taste. Can be found, in Middle-Eastern stores, international / gourmet section of some supermarkets; and health food stores.

SERVING: per person 6-8oz.

SPIKE: a seasoning made from a combination of natural herbs and spices. To be found in most supermarkets and health food stores. Before purchasing, it is recommended to review the ingredients, to make sure they agree with you.

TOFU: most recipes in t his book been prepared with firm tofu. You might like to experiment, which tofu you like best. To remove excess moisture, squeeze tofu in a thick paper towel. After package is opened change water daily.
❤to❤

INDEX

Almondto Pudding 59
B. B. Q Tofu 36
Baked Potato Topping 5
Banana & Tofu for Babies 2
Bean & Tofu Dip 6
Bread Crumbs 3
Burritos 37
Carrot & Tofu Salad 16
Chili Sauce 31
Chocolate T Mint Pudding 60
Corn & Tofu Mush 38
Cottage Cheese & Tofu Filling 27
Cranberry & Tofu Gelatin 61
Cream of Wheat & Tofu 39
Cucumber-Tofu Salad 17
Curry & Tofu Chowder 40
Egg & Tofu Salad 18
Enchilada Filling 28
Enchilada Sauce 32
Flaedle Suppe 13
(soup, german style)
Fruit Salad Dressing 26
(TOFRUITY)
Garbanto Patty 41
Guacamole I. 7
Guacamole II. 8
Hummus 9
Italian dressing 25
Kartoffel Puffer 42
(potato puffs, german style
Lasagne Filling 29
Lasagne Sauce 33
Meerrettich Sosse 34
(horseradish sauce, germans style)
Mushroom-Tofu Filling 30
Mushroom & Tofu Marinade 19
Mushroom-Tofu Patty 43
Omelet 44
Onion-Tofu dip 10
Parmesan a la Tofu 45
Pasta & Tofu Salad 20
Peanutto Spread 11
Pie Crust 4
Pfannenkuchen I. 46
(pancakes, german style)
Pfannenkuchen II. 47
Quiche 48
Recipe for Happiness 1
Rote Rueben & Tofu Salat, 21
(beet salad, german style)
Rot Kraut & Tofu 49
(red cabbage, german style)
Salzkartoffel 50
(potatoes, german style)
Sauerkraut & Tofu 51
(suaerkraut, german style)
Scrambled Eggs & Tofu 52
Sesame-Tofu Patty 53
Stir Fry 54
Tabule 22
(tabouli, lebanese style)
Tartar Sauce 35
(with tofu)
Tart'ly Tofu 23
Tofu-Cheese Ball 12
Tofu Cutlet 55
Tomato Soup I. 14
Tomato Soup II. 15
Tomato & Tofu Salad 24
Tortillas Excelente 56
Vanilla-Tofu Pudding 62
Yam & Tofu Delight 57
Zucchini & Tofu Casserole 58

CATEGORY

Miscellaneous

Recipe for Happiness 1
Banana & Tofu for Babies 2
Bread Crumbs 3
Pie Crust 4

Dips & Spreads

Baked Potato Topping 5
Bean & Tofu Dip 6
Guacamole I. 7
Guacamole II. 8
Hummus 9
Onion-Tofu Dip 10
Peanutto Spread 11
Tofu-Cheese Ball 12

Soups

Flaedle Suppe 13
Tomato Soup I. 14
Tomato Soup II. 15

Salads

Carrot & Tofu Salad 16
Cucumber-Tofu Salad 17
Egg & Tofu Salad 18
Mushroom & Tofu Marinade 19
Pasta & Tofu Salad 20
Rote Rueben & Tofu Salat 21
Tabule 22
Tart'ly Tofu 23
Tomato & Tofu Salad 24

Salad Dressing

Italian Dressing 25
Fruit Salad Dressing 26

Filling

Cottage cheese & Tofu Filling 27
Enchilada Filling 28
Lasagne Filling 29
Mushroom-Tofu Filling 30

Sauces

Chili Sauce 31
Enchilada Sauce 32
Lasagne Sauce 33
Meerrettich Sosse 34
Tartar Sauce 35

Main Dish

B. B. Q Tofu 36
Burritos 37
Corn & Tofu Mush 38
Cream of Wheat & Tofu 39
Curry & Tofu Chowder 40
Garbanto Patty 41
Kartoffel Puffer 42
Mushroom-Tofu Patty 43
Omelet 44
Parmesan a la Tofu 45
Pfannenkuchen I. 46
Pfannenkuchen II. 47
Quiche 48
Rot Kraut & Tofu 49
Salzkartoffel 50
Sauerkraut & Tofu 51
Scrambled Eggs & Tofu 52
Sesame-Tofu Patty 53
Stir fry 54
Tofu Cutlet 55
Tortillas Excelente 56
Yam & Tofu Delight 57
Zucchini & Tofu Casserole 58

Desserts

Almondto Pudding 59
Chocolate T Mint Pudding 60
Cranberry & Tofu Gelatin 61
Vanilla -Tofu Pudding 62